Learn With Animals

In the Arctic

By Laura Ottina
Adapted by Barbara Bakowski

Illustrated by
Sebastiano Ranchetti

WEEKLY READER®
PUBLISHING

We live in the Arctic
On hard, frozen ground,
And in icy-cold waters
We swim around.

3

I am a puffin,

All black and white

Except for my beak,

Which is very bright.

6

I am an Arctic wolf
With a white, furry coat.
I let out a loud howl
From deep in my throat.

I am a musk ox
With long, shaggy hair.
My coat keeps me warm
In the cold Arctic air.

9

10

I am a harp seal,
A swimmer so skilled.
I have thick blubber
So I never feel chilled.

I am a reindeer.
I wear antlers quite showy.
My big hooves leave prints
On ground that is snowy.

13

14

I am an orca,
A very fast swimmer.
I use my sharp teeth
To eat fish for dinner.

I am a polar bear.
My fur is pure white.
Over high piles of snow
I climb with delight.

17

I am a grouse,
A bird with brown feathers
That turn snowy white
In winter's cold weather.

I am a lemming
Fat, furry, and small.
When winter comes,
Into my burrow I crawl.

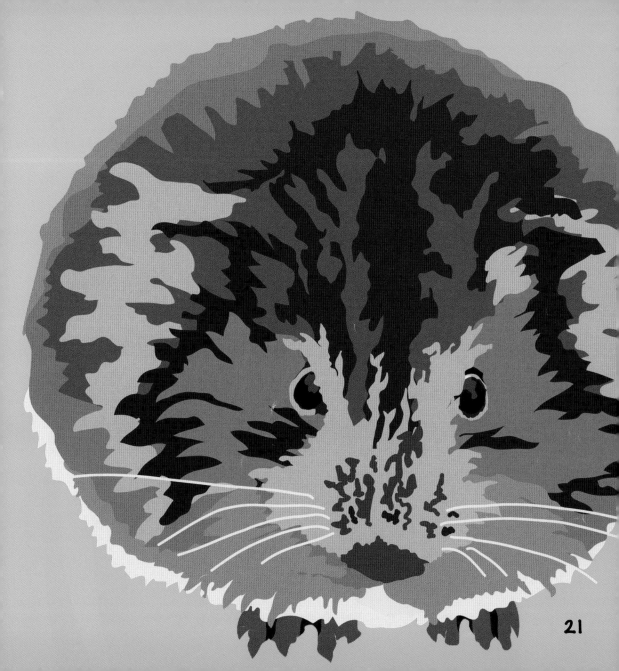

21

I am a walrus.
My tusks are quite nice.
I use them as hooks
To climb onto the ice.

Please visit our web site at **www.garethstevens.com**.
For a free catalog describing our list of high-quality books,
call 1-800-542-2595 (USA) or 1-800-387-3178 (Canada).
Our fax: 1-877-542-2596

Library of Congress Cataloging-in-Publication Data
Ottina, Laura.
  [Incontra gli animali nell'Artico. English]
  In the Arctic / by Laura Ottina ; adapted by Barbara Bakowski ;
illustrated by Sebastiano Ranchetti.
    p. cm. – (Learn with animals)
  ISBN-10: 1-4339-1911-7   ISBN-13: 978-1-4339-1911-4 (lib. bdg.)
  ISBN-10: 1-4339-2088-3   ISBN-13: 978-1-4339-2088-2 (softcover)
  1. Animals–Arctic regions–Juvenile literature.   I. Bakowski, Barbara.
II. Ranchetti, Sebastiano, ill.   III. Title.
  QL105.08813   2010
  591.70911'–dc22   2008052365

This North American edition first published in 2010 by
Weekly Reader® Books
An Imprint of Gareth Stevens Publishing
1 Reader's Digest Road
Pleasantville, NY 10570-7000 USA

This U.S. edition copyright © 2010 by Gareth Stevens, Inc. International Copyright
© 2008 by Editoriale Jaca Book spa, Milan, Italy. All rights reserved. First published
in 2008 as *Incontra gli animali nell'Artico* by Editoriale Jaca Book spa.

Gareth Stevens Executive Managing Editor: Lisa M. Herrington
Gareth Stevens Senior Editor: Barbara Bakowski
Gareth Stevens Creative Director: Lisa Donovan
Gareth Stevens Designer: Jennifer Ryder-Talbot

Printed in the United States of America

1 2 3 4 5 6 7 8 9 12 11 10 09

Find out more about Laura Ottina and Sebastiano Ranchetti at **www.animalsincolor.com**.